DATE DUE

JUNGLES

ANDREW LANGLEY

The Bookwright Press
New York · 1987

Topics

The Age of the Dinosaur
Ancient Peoples
Bridges
Castles
Earthquakes and Volcanoes
Energy
Farm Animals
Great Disasters
Houses and Homes
Inventions
Jungles

Maps and Globes
Money
Peoples of the World
Photography
Pollution and Conservation
Religions
Robots
Spacecraft
Television
Trees of the World
Under the Ground

All the words that appear
in **bold** are explained in the
glossary on page 30.

First published in
the United States in 1987 by
The Bookwright Press
387 Park Avenue South
New York, NY 10016

First published in 1986 by
Wayland (Publishers) Ltd
61 Western Road, Hove
East Sussex BN3 1JD

© Copyright 1986 Wayland (Publishers) Ltd

ISBN 0–531–18111–1
Library of Congress Catalog Card Number: 86–70971

Phototypeset by
Kalligraphics Ltd, Redhill, Surrey
Printed in Belgium
by Casterman S.A.

Contents

In the Jungle   4

Plants of the Rainforest   9

The Hunters and the Hunted   14

The Jungle People   20

The Vanishing Forests   26

Glossary   30

Books to Read   31

Index   32

In the Jungle

Imagine you are at the edge of a jungle. To get inside you have to hack a way through thick tangles of creepers and vines. Once you are past these, the going becomes easier. All around, huge trees tower up into a mass of **foliage** high above. The **canopy** of leaves forms a sunshade, blocking out most of the light and allowing few smaller plants to grow on the forest floor.

The canopy does not keep out the heat. The air is stiflingly hot and there is no breeze. It is also very **humid**, for thunderstorms bring torrents of rain each day. As much as 500 mm (20 in) may fall in one day, and in the wettest areas 4,000 mm (160 in) fall in a year.

For this reason jungles are usually called **rainforests**. They lie within the **tropics**, where the sun is hottest and the rainfall is highest.

The towering trees of the Amazon jungle create dark and humid conditions on the forest floor.

4

The largest rainforest covers the basins of the Amazon and Orinoco Rivers in South America. Farther east, in Africa, jungle grows along the Zaire River. The third great belt of rainforest is in Southeast Asia, stretching from Burma to New Guinea.

Jungles provide perfect conditions in which plants can

The world's rainforests lie within the Tropics of Cancer and Capricorn, around the Equator.

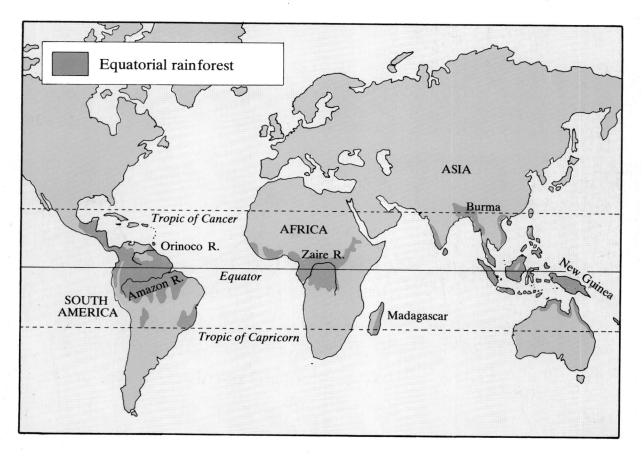

Equatorial rainforest

ASIA

Burma

Tropic of Cancer

AFRICA

Orinoco R.

Zaire R.

Equator

Amazon R.

New Guinea

SOUTH
AMERICA

Madagascar

Tropic of Capricorn

Ideal growing conditions allow many plants and trees to thrive in the rainforests.

thrive. Within a small area there may be over 200 different kinds of large trees, some of which grow as high as 45 m (150 ft). On them and below them grow huge numbers of flowers, climbers, ferns, mosses and **fungi**.

The jungle is both home and hunting ground for a great variety of animals. Up in the canopy live birds, monkeys, squirrels and even frogs. The shady floor provides food for pigs, **rodents** and large **predators** such as tigers and

A tiger, the largest of the jungle predators, watches for game in a forest clearing.

Some jungle insects are very unusual, like this strange-looking stick insect.

panthers. And everywhere there are insects. Nobody knows for certain how many different **species** of insects live in the rainforest, but scientists believe there may be more than 20 million.

Plants of the Rainforest

In order to grow, plants need light, water and food, which they obtain from the warm, wet jungle. But there are so many plants in the jungle that only the strongest get enough food and water to grow fully. Their smaller rivals have to

The forest giants tower above the other trees in the jungle.

The forest giants are often top-heavy, so they grow huge buttress roots to support them.

make the best of what is left.

The tall trees take most of the light. Their slender trunks are bare to the height of 20 m (65 ft) from the ground. They then branch out into a flat **crown** of leaves, forming an almost unbroken layer of greenery over the forest. Here and there even bigger trees rise above the canopy. These are the giants, often 10 m (32 ft) higher than their neighbors, but fewer in number.

But these trees are not very secure. Their roots are shallow and give little support. If their crowns get too heavy the trees may keel over in a storm. To prevent this, some species have developed special **buttress roots**, which fan out from the trunk and prop it up.

It is not only the leaves that weigh down the trees. From below grow the climbers, which use other plants for support. Some of these send out roots that take nourishment from the trees. Others

Some climbers become so large that they eventually strangle their host trees.

smother their **hosts** with leaves, starving them of sunlight and eventually killing them.

There are other types of hanging plants. Orchids, ferns and

bromeliads grow in cracks in the tree trunks and along branches. They have no roots in the ground, but get the food they need from the decaying leaves that fall onto them from above. Some even catch and store rainwater in their cup-shaped leaves.

Down on the forest floor, very few plants find enough light or food to survive. Vast numbers of dead leaves fall and are broken down in the heat and moisture with great

Bromeliads grow on the branches of the trees, and depend on falling leaves for their food.

speed. A single leaf may rot in less than two months: in northern forests, this process might take a year.

The rotting process is carried out by fungi and other **parasites**, whose tiny threads can break down even the toughest leaves. The most spectacular parasite is the rafflesia. This produces the largest single flower of any plant – up to 90 cm (3 ft) across – and gives off a powerful smell of rotting meat.

The huge flower of the rafflesia plant gives off a very strong smell.

The Hunters and the Hunted

Many people imagine the jungle to be a noisy place, with fierce creatures lurking at every step. In fact, during the heat of the day, it can be very quiet. You are not likely to spot many animals unless you have great patience or can climb trees. For it is high up in the forest canopy that most jungle creatures are to be found.

This squirrel monkey uses its strong limbs and tail to swing through the branches of the jungle trees.

The orangutan lives in the forests of Sumatra and Borneo; its name means "man of the woods."

The biggest and noisiest are the monkeys. They are perfectly adapted to life in the trees, and few venture down to the ground. Using their long limbs and clutching fingers they can swing from branch to branch at great speed. The orangutan, for instance, is 1.5 m (5 ft) tall, yet the span of its arms is 2.4 m (8 ft). The gibbon also has long arms, and travels so fast that it can leap across gaps of 6 m (20 ft).

The canopy is also home to a great number of birds, each with its own special way of eating. Beautifully colored parrots use their bills as nutcrackers. The large beaks of toucans and hornbills can pluck and toss fruit into their mouths with amazing skill. Tiny hummingbirds hover over jungle flowers, sucking out the **nectar** through their long thin beaks.

This red-billed hornbill has caught a large insect in its strong beak.

Other animals have adapted to moving through the trees. The paradise tree snake solves the problem by gliding from branch to branch. It flattens its ribs and steers itself through the air with swimming movements. Lizards, lemurs and frogs can also glide, using special flaps of skin between their legs and toes.

A flying frog perches on a leaf, ready to glide away.

Some creatures make regular trips from the forest floor to the canopy. Acacia ants live in large colonies on the acacia tree, whose flowers provide them with nectar, and in return they defend the tree, attacking other insects and killing climbing plants.

Big cats also climb trees in search of food. The clouded leopard hunts monkeys and squirrels, which it swipes to the ground with its paws. The jaguar ambushes deer and other game by dropping from the

A leopard carries its cub down to the forest floor.

branches onto their backs. Once their stomachs are full, these cats climb up again into the trees to find a comfortable place to sleep.

The deadly bushmaster snake lives in the tropical rainforests of South America.

Many more fearsome killers live on the forest floor or in the jungle rivers. The most deadly of them is the bushmaster snake. It grows to 3.6 m (12 ft) long and its poison can kill a full grown human being. One terrible killer is the piranha fish. A shoal of them can tear a large animal to pieces in minutes.

The Jungle People

Humans have lived in the rainforest for a very long time. They have learned to make the best use of its rich resources. Over the centuries, their bodies have become specially suited to its heat and humidity.

Jungle people are able to stay cool in the heat of the forest. There is little hair on their bodies and they do not sweat very much. Because they work hard and lead an outdoor life, they are usually fit and healthy.

They are also smaller than people living in cold climates. The Pygmies of Zaire are rarely more than 1.5 m (4 ft 9 in) tall. This makes it easy for them to move swiftly and silently among the trees in pursuit of game.

The Pygmies are wanderers, living in bands of twenty or more. They are very skillful hunters, using

Pygmy women fetch water from a stream near their camp.

bows and arrows to shoot birds, or nets and spears to capture deer. They even hunt elephants, wounding them and leaving them to die. Later they return and cut up the body so they can carry it back to camp.

A Pygmy boy puts away nets, which the hunters use for catching animals.

An Amazonian Indian sets off on a hunting expedition with his bow and arrows.

The hunters of the Amazon use **blowpipes** as well as bows and arrows. They coat the tips of their darts with poison obtained from frogs. With these blowpipes they can hit a bird nearly 30m (98 ft) above them in the trees.

Not all the jungle people are simple **nomads**. The Dyaks of Borneo build wooden **longhouses** for their families. They clear small areas of jungle, chopping and burning the trees. They then plant crops, such as rice, corn and bananas. After two or three years, the soil becomes exhausted and a new clearing must be made.

The Dyaks of Borneo live in small village communities in wooden longhouses.

The Indians of the Amazon build their houses on stilts to avoid the floods.

Some South American tribes build their villages on the banks of the Amazon River. The floods, which occur once a year, leave fertile mud in which good crops may be grown. The food has to be dried and stored before the next flood arrives. The river peoples also kill fish, water birds, turtles and even crocodiles for food.

An Amazonian fisherman casts his net in the hope of catching some fish.

The Vanishing Forests

The jungle peoples have lived in harmony with the jungle for hundreds of years. They take from it only food, shelter and clothing. They have plenty of space for hunting and farming without disturbing the other jungle inhabitants.

But the jungles are being disturbed by people of other countries. Huge numbers of trees are cut down, and the timber is used

The large-scale destruction of the rainforest for industrial purposes poses a serious threat to its survival.

for making paper and other goods. Now that most of the northern forests have been felled the great trees of the rainforests are being cut down.

Modern foresters do not use axes and fire. Instead, they bring in bulldozers and tractors, which can pull down trees with great speed. In order to bring these machines to the rainforests, roads are built, and these cause a great deal of damage. Every year, huge areas of jungle are destroyed.

Modern foresters use powerful machinery to pull down the trees of the jungle.

Latex is taken from a rubber tree in a plantation that used to be jungle.

There are many other reasons why the forests are cut down. People want more farmland to grow food for themselves and their livestock. Land may be used to grow important crops such as rubber and cocoa, which bring much-needed money for the governments of countries like Malaysia. Many tourists visit these areas, which creates a need for roads and hotels.

Once a large area of jungle has been cleared, it will not grow again for many years. When the cover of the great trees has gone, the soil quickly becomes useless. The heavy rains wash out all the topsoil and cause **erosion**.

The destruction of the rainforests affects animals as badly as it does plants. Already, many species have become extinct. Others, such as the mountain gorilla and the orang-utan, are also in danger of disappearing for ever.

Saddest of all is the decline of the jungle peoples. Many have been driven out as the forests are cut down. They live unhappily in towns nearby, and easily catch diseases such as influenza and measles, from which they often die. Before it is too late, we need to find a way of preserving the jungle and its great natural wealth.

Once the jungle has been destroyed, soil erosion occurs and few new plants manage to grow.

Glossary

Blowpipe A tube of bamboo or reed through which a dart is blown.

Bromeliads Tropical plants, of the pineapple family, which grow on the trunks and branches of jungle trees.

Buttress roots Projecting growths that help to support the trunks of jungle trees.

Canopy The upper layer of leaves in the rainforest formed by the tall trees.

Crown The leaves and upper branches of a tree.

Erosion The washing away of the top layer of soil by rains and streams.

Foliage The leaves of growing plants.

Fungi Soft, spongy growths, many of which grow on rotting wood.

Hosts Animals or plants that are food and support for parasites.

Humid Moist or damp.

Latex The milky juice of the rubber tree, which is collected and used for making rubber products.

Longhouses Long wooden buildings used as dwellings by the forest peoples of Borneo and New Guinea.

Nectar The sweet liquid produced by flowers, which is gathered by birds and insects for food.

Nomads Tribes that have no fixed settlement, and wander over a wide area in search of food.

Parasites Organisms that live on other creatures, and take food and shelter from them.

Predators Animals that live by hunting and eating other animals.

Rainforests The evergreen forests that cover the tropical regions of the world.

Rodents Mammals with front teeth that grow continuously, causing them to nibble and gnaw.

Species A group of animals or plants that are alike in many ways.

Tropics The two imaginary lines around the globe that mark the boundaries of the hot equatorial region.

Books to Read

Bains, Rae. *Forests and Jungles.* Mahwah, NJ: Troll Associates, 1985.

Catchpole, Clive. *Jungles.* New York: Dial Books for Young Readers, 1984.

Cheney, Glenn Alan. *The Amazon.* New York: Franklin Watts, 1984.

Eden, Michael. *Rain Forests.* Bridgeport, CT: Merrimack Publishing Corp., 1982.

Johnson, Sylvia. *Animals of the Tropical Forests.* Minneapolis, MN: Lerner Publications, 1976.

Newton, James R. *Rain Shadow.* New York: Crowell Junior Books, 1983.

Norden, Carroll. *The Jungle.* Milwaukee, WI: Raintree Childrens Books, 1983.

Pope, Joyce. *A Closer Look at Jungles, rev. ed.* New York: Franklin Watts, 1984.

Picture Acknowledgments

The pictures in this book were supplied by: J Allan Cash 25; Camerapix Hutchison Library 20, 21, 22; Bruce Coleman Ltd, by the following photographers: A Compost 13, 28, 29; M Fogden 12, 19, cover; F Lanting 9; O A J Mobbs 17; N Myers 26; D & M Plage 18; G D Plage 7; M P Price 15; G Ziesler 8, 14, 16; C Zuber 27; Marion Morrison/South American Pictures 24; Tony Morrison/South American Pictures 4, 6, 10, 11; Malcolm Walker 5; Wayland Picture Library 23.

Index

Animals 7–8, 14–9

Birds 7, 13, 16
  Hornbills 13, 16
  Hummingbirds 16
  Parrots 16
  Toucans 16
Burma 5
Buttress roots 10

Canopy 4, 10, 14, 16

Diseases 29

Erosion 28

Farming 23, 24, 26, 28
Fish 19, 25
Foresters 27–8
Fungi 6

Gliding animals 17

Houses 23, 24
Hunting 20–22

Insects 8, 18

Jungle, destruction of 27–8
Jungle people 20–25, 26
  Dyaks of Borneo 23
  Hunters of the Amazon 22

Pygmies of Zaire 20–21

Malaysia 28
Monkeys 7, 14, 15, 18, 28
  Gibbon 15
  Mountain gorilla 28
  Orangutan 15, 28
  Squirrel monkey 14

New Guinea 5

Parasites 13
Plants 5, 9–13
  Bromeliads 12
  Climbers 6, 10, 11
Predators 7, 8, 18
  Jaguar 18
  Leopard 18
  Panther 8
  Tiger 7

Rivers 5, 6, 20, 22, 24

Snakes 17, 19
South America 5
Southeast Asia 5

Tourists 28
Towns 29
Trees 10–11
Tropics 4